HOW TO BOUNCE

Copyright

ISBN: 9798838866981

All Rights Reserved.

Maxine A. Robinson

Dedication

I dedicate this book to my son Bakari Ani Robinson. He has been my "WHY" in writing this book. I want to show him that with principles and strength he can be an overcomer regardless of any situation he may experience in his lifetime. I love you, Bakari.

Momma

About the Author

Maxine Robinson is from Cincinnati, Ohio, a city in the Midwest; however, her roots run from the Mississippi River to the Ohio River. Cincinnati is a quiet town with a far slower pace of living than big cities like New York or Washington, DC. and is known for being a great place to raise a family. Unconsciously, she wanted what most women wanted, and that was to be married and to raise a family, maybe larger than hers when she was growing up because she had only one sibling, a younger sister. Maxine did not really realize this until she began to write this book after discovering she was tormented by the loss of her marriage which she felt was a huge part of her identity. However, she later learned after she healed from the divorce that the desire was only one facet of her identity. She realized she had many facets, and marriage was just one of them which did not make her whole. It was, in fact, OK to go through the loss because it was an experience that makes her who she is today, a resilient, strong, empathetic woman. Maxine brings insights on the experience of divorce. She wants to share with her readers how she was able to mentally hold herself together during and after the divorce.

About the Book

The book provides strategies on how to overcome a relationship loss with interactive activities which are designed to show how you can peel back layers of yourself to overcome a loss. While peeling back the layers, you are able to discern if you had any control of the loss and how you can take a negative experience and turn it into a positive experience in order to build a solid foundation for a strong recovery.

The author wants to give the readers a fresh insight into their lives, bringing about a burst of energy to continue living with a stronger purpose. The readers will be able to gain a new strategic purpose which allows them to be their authentic selves and become the best persons they can be to themselves without compromise.

Table of Contents

CHAPTER 1 ……………..Accept the Loss…………………….....8

CHAPTER 2……………. Seek Counseling ……………………..10

CHAPTER 3…….........Cut the Umbilical cord…………………12

CHAPTER 4………. …Focus on Yourself……………………..16

CHAPTER 5…………. Declutter your Spaces ………………..21

CHAPTER 6…………Take Charge of Your Finances………   31

CHAPTER 7…………. Accept Accountability……....................37

CHAPTER 8…………. Trigger…………………………………..41

CHAPTER 9……………Control your Emotions……………….47

CHAPTER 10. ……… Don't Feel Invisible……… ……………..53

CHAPTER 11 …………Exert Confidence……………………….59

CHAPTER 12…………Affirm Yourself…,…............................64

CHAPTER 13. ………   Limit Your Usage of social media ..…..67

CHAPTER 14…………., Do Not Compromise Yourself ………75

CHAPTER 15…………Be Content…....……………………..81

CHAPTER 16 ………Live Vibrantly……………………… .83

CHAPTER 17……........Enjoy Friendships……...……………92

CHAPTER 18… Establish a New Relationship Cautiously…....99

CHAPTER 19 Give Thanks 108 ..CHAPTER 20 My Prayer..113

CHAPTER ONE

Accept the Loss

The first thing you must do is accept the loss. In order for acceptance, you must take a personal assessment of yourself to determine what you need most in your life and what you want in the next stage of your life. Many times, a loss can be closure of one door to the opening of a new door with more opportunities; therefore, you should embrace it and accept the change. I am not saying this action is easy, but it is a step of accepting a loss and stepping into your truth.

Take time to think about what you will miss because of the loss. How happy were you prior to the loss? Look at yourself to determine if there's something you can do to be better as a result of this loss so you can correct any mistakes or hardships that may have caused the loss.

I now want to tell you my experience and loss in my lifetime, which was so dear to my heart. I want to share what I learned and offer some tips that got me over the hump, that made me whole and happy. I was able to keep my swag and motivation to persevere without missing a beat.

When my husband no longer talked to me on a regular basis, such as having a daily conversation, I then realized he was no longer mine. When he didn't take me out on dates or other outings, such as family or work-related events, especially when we were married, he was totally gone emotionally. When he had absolutely nothing positive to say to me and consistently appeared to be always stressed and acted as if I was irritating him, this is when I realized he definitely had no interest in my existence. I know this sounds harsh, but this was my reality. When this happened, I sat into my reality, which did not feel comfortable. However, once I did, I became aligned with my acceptance of what was then my situation

CHAPTER TWO

Seek Counseling

Mental health wellness is vital when getting over a loss. It's common for people to seek help after a loss, such as a divorce, and although I am not a professional counselor, I would recommend one. When I was going through my divorce, I sought out a counselor. I wanted to be able to speak to someone confidentially about my problems. I wanted to air out all my issues with someone who did not know me and could be transparent providing advice of what I needed to do without judgment.

While on my search for a counselor, I found out I could have up to six free sessions, as well as other members in my household under the Employee Assistance Program (EAP) offered through my employer. I was happy for the free sessions because the average cost for an hour session was $120 for a licensed mental health counselor or psychiatrist.

My counselor provided me with strategies and ideas during my loss with next action steps. My sessions helped me tremendously. I went to counseling for 10 consecutive weeks. I was able to get my additional 4 weeks approved for free as well.

The mental health counseling was the best investment I had ever taken advantage of in my lifetime. The opportunity to sit with someone speaking transparently and confidentially is a powerful strategy when recovering from a loss. After my sessions, I no longer felt empty or alone but felt fulfilled. My sessions created healing and a sense of empowerment.

CHAPTER THREE

Cut the Umbilical Cord

I told myself to face the fact that he is no longer into you and prepare yourself for the break by doing self-healing. When he told me he no longer wanted to be married to me, this was the perfect opportunity for me to cut the umbilical cord symbolically speaking – to detach myself from the relationship. I then had to let God handle the rest and just stand.

At that moment, the news was devastating to me, and I felt as if my heart had been ripped out of my chest. I later believed this experience was one of the best things that had ever happened in my life. So, I began the process of self-healing, learning, reflecting, and thinking about what I could have done better as a person. The old saying "It takes two to tango" represents that both parties are at fault; no one is innocent.

Are you ready to cut the umbilical cord and begin your self-healing? Are you ready to see just what you're made of? Are you ready to walk into your destiny to overcome your loss?

You may have felt stuck before you began to read this book, but you should know you're not because that feeling is only a mindset. Just step out on faith and cut the umbilical cord. You have to love yourself more than anything with extreme confidence, knowing you'll succeed in whatever you have the passion to do. Today, I challenge you as I challenge myself consistently with tenacity to live your life with freedom. Get out of the familiar, being comfortable, and get uncomfortable. When you step out of the familiar, it's a sign that you're about to give birth to something new in your life. Never give up when things feel uncomfortable.

Life is such a grandstand as we travel through time by the second, minute, and hour of the day; we never know what kind of curve ball life is going to throw at us. Don't fret, just take a deep breath, acknowledge what is happening, and tackle it. Don't get nervous or overwhelmed. Just remember you can only control yourself by your actions and emotions. You can't control others or situations outside of your scope when, in fact, you have no control of their decisions.

I say to you, don't spend your time or energy worrying about something you absolutely have no control over as you begin to self-heal. For example, recently, I lost my driver's license. I looked everywhere; it was nowhere to be found. Even though I wasn't in control of the license reappearing, I was able to control my emotions by not getting upset and having the situation take over my mind, body, and mood. I told myself, "Ok, you lost your driver's license; there's nothing you can do to make it reappear." At that moment, I made a decision to stop looking and made plans to get another one. I made a decision not to waste valuable time on something beyond my control when that time could be used on something more tangible.

This is a clear example of creating a strategy for overcoming a situation which could have otherwise caused a great amount of stress. Learning how to strategize various issues that may arise is important when moving forward and makes staying focused on our goals without any distractions easy.

Strategizing a resolution to a situation hasn't always been easy for me; I had to first learn how to connect with my emotions. I now take the temperature of my emotions and answer questions, such as "How are you feeling or are you overwhelmed?" After taking inventory of my emotions, I determine if I'm getting a return on my investment (ROI). If the answer is no, I don't spend any time on the issue, a task, or an individual. I keep moving forward with positivity dripping all over my body of armor.

When life throws you a curveball and you've strategized a resolution, let go of the things that you have no control over. When I say let it go, let it go! Free your mind and continue to move forward.

CHAPTER FOUR

Focus on Yourself

Focus on yourself to discern what in life you still want to accomplish despite a failed relationship or your loss. Take inventory of your life and figure out what you really want to accomplish. How do you want your life to be going forward? It's time to set new goals and prioritize them one piece at a time; it's like a puzzle. It's best to start with one thing and focus on that one thing so you can accomplish your goals, maximizing results. If you start on more than one thing at a time, you will not finish anything; as a result, you will only become frustrated.

Think for a moment that you have 1,440 minutes in a day. You spend approximately 480 minutes sleeping and another 480 minutes working; that's if you have a 9 to 5 job, totaling 960 minutes. You are now left with 480 minutes, which half of that time may be divided into taking care of a loved one, such as a child, or being a caregiver to a parent. Now that leaves you with 240 minutes to yourself which is a full 4 hours. Wow, 4 hours is a lot of time to work on your desired goals.

Think for a moment that during the week, most people like myself may have only 1 job, maybe 2; however, somewhere during the week, you may have a couple of days off. Wow, that gives you 1,440 minutes to yourself which is a whole 4 hours. What will you work on consistently to manifest your passions?

Make a commitment to yourself. Limit your time from electronics and really concentrate on your whole well-being. Practice making the 240-rule a habit, and you will experience growth with positive outcomes.

What is the one thing you like to do or would like to do that sparks your interest? What is the one thing today that gives you extreme joy and pleasure and fulfills your passion? My personal passion is working out. I get emotional in my workouts because they relieve my stress. While working out, I have clarity in my thought process surrounding my goals. I also process my to-do-list for the day. I'm also able to brainstorm new ideas, which are refreshing to my soul. This is easy because I don't have busyness in my head. During this period, I take time to reflect on where I'm at in my life and where I want to go.

If you find your passion, work on it every chance you get. This will make your life whole, especially when dealing with the loss; you will have clarity and will be able to recognize your needs. You'll be able to get over the loss and make more desirable plans for yourself. This process will further brighten your future.

Don't over think! Practice and build on your desired passion. As Nike says," Just Do It!" If you don't act on your passion now, another day, week, month, and year will go by. You'll later regret the time you lost because the one thing we can never get back is time.

Once you discover your passion, operate in it. You'll discover you actually could have never known acting on your passion could have brought you so much gratification mentally, physically, emotionally, and financially.

I say to you don't wait another second, minute, or hour in a day. Act on your passion today. Working on your passion is the best gift you can ever give yourself in life while you're living. Leave your legacy; stamp your footprint in this world. If you don't, it'll be another lost dream buried away.

God would not want us to neglect our passions because it is He who gave us life to fulfill our purpose. Someone once said if we aren't acting in our purpose and destiny, it's like slapping God in the face because by having His DNA we need to be like Him or better than He was during His lifetime.

List Your Passion

CHAPTER FIVE

Declutter Your Spaces

Have you ever felt like you're just existing? When I say just existing, I mean doing daily routines, such as working, maintaining your household for the family, and paying bills.

Recently, I realized that in my years of my living, I was just existing after my divorce. I came to this conclusion one day when I was clearing out some clutter in my basement storage closet which I hadn't touched in years since my divorce. With the New Year approaching, I had decided to throw out items or give them away. I realized if I hadn't looked at the items in years, it was time they were removed from my household.

After making the decision, I began this task and was blown away by how much I had tucked in this storage closet. I was ashamed of myself because I could have just given the items to someone or the thrift store years ago. I questioned why I was holding on to these items. There were chairs, a coffee table, and even a printer. It made absolutely no sense. Did I keep storing items in this closet because I was too lazy to make the proper placement or get rid of them? Maybe that was the case. But, for whatever reason, when removing the items, I had an Ah Ha moment. I realized that I had just been holding onto items from the past that I had tucked away. As I began to remove the items, I felt tears welling up, but I refused to have self-pity by crying. I sucked it up and came to grips that I really hadn't been well mentally for years during the separation and after the divorce, and the fact that I had been tucking things away was evidence of that behavior.

    I ask you today have you tucked things away, not taking the time to store them in their proper place or taking the time to give the items away since the loss of your relationship. Set aside some time today and take inventory of the spaces in your home. Where are those spaces in your home? Are there items tucked in boxes, by your bed, in drawers or closets? Take some time and think about these spaces, plan a time when you will tackle this chore, and then start moving or removing the items.

    I can say I didn't set this task on my calendar, but it had been in my thought process for months. I would think about it, and then I would say I'll do it the following week. But because the New Year was approaching, I woke up one Sunday morning and said today is the day, and I began the process.

    I also realize that the behavior that I had done over the years had become part of my character which was tucking things away, not taking the time to fully deal with what was in front of me by saying I'll deal with it later. Just writing about this incident has been therapeutic because I could see that I just hadn't been dealing with my reality of being divorced which truly kept me from overcoming some things in my life that I've had to let go.

What are you holding on to? What are you not letting go because you have been hanging on to items in your home that should have been disposed of years ago?

List Your Tuck-Away Spaces

What Items Did You Find?

How Do the Items Make You feel?

Now that you have removed these items, do you feel some relief? After clearing away the clutter, do you think you were carrying any burdens? Due to you now clearing cluttered spaces, you should feel some type of relief or clarity in your environment. You should have a smile on your face knowing you have acknowledged the clutter that was tucked away. Maybe these were items you had to dispose, fix, or give away. Whatever the case was, you have cleared the spaces of clutter from the past that was in your home. This task will help you while getting over your loss because you are now able to move forward. Squeeze and pat yourself on the back because I know just getting the items removed or put in their proper placement in your home was work but rewarding work.

After I removed the items, I noticed how the home scenery was still in place after my ex-spouse's departure. For example, the curtains, paint, and even the decorations were still the same throughout the house. It was if he had never left, even though he was gone physically. I had unconsciously left things as they were, not noticing I was still holding on to physical objects we shared. After my Ah Ha moment, I decided it was time for a bigger change, not just removing items from the basement, but items tucked away in dark places. My entire home needed a makeover. Changes were not just needed with me physically and emotionally, but my home environment needed a change. I painted the walls and removed dated furniture.

 If you want to move forward and beyond the feeling of just existing after the loss, begin to take inventory of what changes you need to make in your home environment, such as the ones I mentioned. Start with small changes. It's understandable that they can't be done overnight, but you can begin to make the shift for new things in your space that will add value after removing the past clutter from a loss such as a divorce.

List Changes You Will Make to Your Environment

CHAPTER SIX

Take Charge of Your Finances

What is the condition of your finances today? I have found that when you know the condition of your finances, it's less of a distraction when recovering from a loss, particularly if the one you lost was a financial supporter in your life. The person may have been paying 50-100% of the expenses, and now you are responsible for 100% of the expenses. If you're overwhelmed with bills, you'll become stressed and unable to move forward with your recovery, but if you know how to manage your finances, you'll feel secure and optimistic about moving forward.

To begin to know the condition of your finances, if you have no idea, may feel painful. Start today and begin keeping a record showing your spending habits for items or services. While keeping a record, also write down your monthly expenses and then prepare a budget. By keeping a record of your spending habits, you'll become aware of your expenses and will easily identify waste. You'll also get a full picture of what your current income allows for your expenses. After you review your expenses, take a moment, and think about how it makes you feel. Are you surprised by what you found? Are you consuming more than your monthly income? If you're consuming more than your monthly income, evaluate the items. Are there some items you can reduce their cost or delete from your list? Are there some spending habits you need to change? This exercise will bring you peace, and you'll be less distracted as you're dealing with a loss. Your financial situation should be the least thing that should be of concern to you. So, what I'm advising is to have your finances in order so you can concentrate on your healing from the loss, and you'll be able to have more income.

After you have reviewed your finances, it's a good idea to review your personal credit or business credit report if you're now going to be fully responsible for your finances. Do you know your personal or business credit score? If you aren't already aware, there are 3 main National Credit Agencies in the United States: TransUnion, Equifax, and Experian. Did you know there are 5 soft touch credit agencies that prepare a report before it's sent to the main 3 reporting credit agencies? They're Lexis Nexis, Sage Scream, ARS, CoreLogic, and Innovis. You want to request these 5 to freeze your credit report because items are sent to them first, and the 3 main credit agencies can't obtain additional information from them when you apply for credit. Did you know you're eligible for one free credit report per year if you're living in the United States? Take charge now and get to know your credit history because a negative credit history and your spending habits can affect your lifestyle. Again, I can't stress this enough. Just knowing your finances helps you move through the loss with ease because you'll not be worried about finances.

Lastly, do you have any savings or investments? It's never too late to start some type of fund. If you're employed by a company, join the Company's 401k plan. If the company doesn't have a 401k plan or you're self-employed, buy an IRA. I've found that purchasing an IRA has a high return just as much as some mutual funds or savings bonds; however, this is just my opinion. I'm not a Licensed Financial Advisor. Before you make any final decisions, do your homework, and see what works best. If you decide to get a mutual fund or savings bonds, be sure to check various fees. Did you know you could acquire brokerage fees up to 3% or more based on the brokerage company that's monitoring your funds? There're ways to avoid certain fees; again, I say do your homework. Don't expect for anyone to tell you upfront.

A great book that helped me with my financial goals when I started studying investments was Tony Robbins' book *Money Matters*. All people should have this book in their library. After reading his book, I was able to gain up to $3,000 more in my 401k employer account within a month just by making some minor changes. At that time, I changed my account to the Russell 300 and the Russell 200. The 300 indicates the top 300 trading companies in the market, and the 200 is the break of the total 500 trading companies in the market, known as the S&P 500. I had no idea I had the power to change my employer account until reading his book. If I ever see Tony Robbins, I'm going to give him a big bear hug of appreciation.

Just being financially healthy removes a great deal of stress, especially for someone who hasn't been born into wealth. When you're aware of your finances, your anxiety levels are extremely low, and you're less depressed. This has been my personal experience. Although I know this now, I didn't know this 20 years ago; however, this is evidence that it's never too late to make small changes that will better your lifestyle today. When your finances are healthy, you're truly healthy. So, I dare you to take the time to review your finances to determine steps you may need to take to improve your finances and start living. It also can make a peaceful transition when you have a loss, especially if the one you lost was a financial contributor in your life.

CHAPTER SEVEN

Accept Accountability

Accountability is taking responsibility for the actions and the decisions you've made. Throughout life, we have always made decisions. Every decision we make has consequences. Based on the decision, it can be a positive or negative outcome. It's always a good practice to accept accountability for what happens to you when applicable. When thinking of a particular loss, such as a relationship, did you do everything that you thought imaginable to avoid losing the relationship? Is there guilt attached to what you have lost? Can you honestly say you took care of that which you lost with kid gloves prior to you losing it? Did you really give 100% effort or show consistency in taking care of it, or did you let it go and become complacent?

For example, think about the relationship people have with their cars. Does your car still appear new from the interior or exterior after you have owned it for 2 years? Do you keep your car nice and clean, smelling good like the first week you purchased it from the dealership? On the other hand, is the car nasty and dirty, rarely getting water and soap applied for the sake of cleaning? Remember how you would wash, wax, and shine your tires with tire cleanser. What about how you would keep the interior of your car? You may have had a rule that no one could eat or drink in your car. Now, what does the car look like today? The interior today may stay cluttered with paper, food particles, water bottles, cans, etc.

Your car then becomes a dumping ground. What happened? When you no longer pamper that which you love, you have truly fallen out of love with it; therefore, you cannot feel bad when you lose it. For example, if you lose your car in an accident, why get upset? You were no longer being appreciative of having it. Likewise, with a relationship, if you don't consistently do the things to maintain a good relationship, it will be lost. When you can accept accountability for your actions that led to the loss of the relationship, you're able to move forward overcoming the loss.

Take a moment and think to yourself, could you have done something better before the loss? Of course, there's something you could've done to prevent the loss. You're now awakened. What are some of your actions that led to the loss of the relationship? For what actions are you accepting accountability?

List 5 or 10 Things That May Have Contributed to the Loss

1.

2.

3.

4.

5.

6.

7.

8.

9.

10.

CHAPTER EIGHT

Manage Triggers

As you're overcoming your loss, you need to manage your triggers, so they don't take over a piece of your happiness. What are triggers? They are anything that can cause an adverse emotional reaction. Triggers can be someone making a statement with which you disagree, imposing on your personal space, or making you extremely agitated. Triggers can affect your positive emotions, which can cause you to act out bad behaviors.

Some people tend to control their mental state of self-consciousness as much as they can; however, if something or someone hits one of their triggers, it can take them off their course of trajectory for a moment. When speaking of trajectory, I mean your focus off a straight path that you may travel on every day. Being off your path can last for a moment, a small period lasting about 24 to 48 hours, or it can last for months. What can we do to recognize our triggers? How do we react to our triggers? Most importantly, how do we keep our triggers from totally derailing us from the path of our goals in life that will manifest our destiny?

Take a moment and think about what triggers your emotions. What makes you do unwanted acts or behaviors? Does someone say something you disagree with, impose on your personal space, or make you extremely agitated? Once you define what causes your triggers, you are better able to keep them under control. For example, you may want to avoid discussing a certain topic or being around certain people who have a different opinion on a controversial topic for an extended period. Just thinking of these two examples, you can put in place coping methods that will prevent a trigger.

I have had situations in which someone may have said something extremely hurtful or done something hurtful, like having a nasty attitude, which has triggered a behavior of overeating. This happens when I have absolutely no control over the situation, which causes the trigger that affects my emotions. As a result, I can sit and eat an entire 24 oz. bag of chips without thinking about the consequences of my actions, like what my scale will show me in the morning. This is a great example of self-sabotage. Now I think before I let a trigger cause one of my bad behaviors such as overeating.

    The worst case of a trigger is when family members trigger a behavior. When this happens, you may feel like they should know better or know the way they are treating you will trigger some type of reaction. However, you know something; they may not even know how their actions are affecting an internal emotion that causes you to perform a behavior or behaviors because of a trigger.

These actions may cause serious harm to you both or other parties. This action can change your mental state and capacity, which you have worked so hard to maintain every day when trying to hold it all together, meaning the things of life you manage every day.

Have you ever taken the time to really think about what and who triggers your emotions to the point that it makes you act out negative behaviors that can sabotage your health and well-being? Please take inventory and meditate on triggers that take you out of your body and make you become someone else or make you behave like someone else, which is not beneficial at all. Even if you justify the action (behavior), it still is not good. Now access a timer. You can use your phone - that's if you have a cell phone nearby - and meditate for 5 to 8 minutes. If you're a skilled meditator, do it for 10 minutes. Try meditating, thinking about what triggers your emotions to make you become uncontrollable in your actions?

Everyone should have that one space to pray, think, or meditate. If you don't have a space, create one. You want a space that is quiet from noise, distraction, or anything that may distract your attention from your goal of meditating.

Where will you make your desired space?

5-8-10

DING

What Triggers Did You Discover?

CHAPTER NINE

Control Your Emotions

Build on a strategy to control your emotions. To overcome a loss, your emotions must be stable. You must be always focused and be aware of your emotions. This may seem hard, but it's not; just think of it as an act of discipline like meditating or praying daily.

Let me now tell you a story about how I learned a lesson of controlling my emotions after my loss. One day I overheard a conversation due to someone not hanging up the phone completely. Instead of me not hanging up the phone, I continued to listen as the individuals were in a conversation with each other. The individuals thought they had hung up the phone, but little did they know their line was still open, and I could hear their conversation.

Has this ever happened to you when you thought you hung up your phone, when in fact your line was still open? I would suggest if it ever happened and you notice the individual didn't hang up, don't linger on the phone line. You may hear something you don't like, or you may interpret the conversation in the wrong manner because you can clearly hear one person dialoguing, but you can only hear the other's response lightly. So, I say to you again don't do it. Hang up! I didn't hang up, and this is what happened. This led to my emotions getting out of control.

The two were doing a comparison of women based on characteristics related to their culture. My culture is totally opposite from their culture. Due to this fact, I felt this is what really enticed me to want to listen; however, I then began to hang on the line.

While on the phone, I picked up some additional insights on how both felt about various cultures. It was as if I had unlocked a hidden code of secrecy. As I listened, I was intrigued by what I heard, so much that I internalized what was said, attaching the comments to myself. I then started to think negatively about myself because some negative comments were made about my culture. I have always felt like a secure woman, but at that moment, the conversation I heard really shook me. Based on my feelings, I began to distance myself without giving my friends notice. I saw them less after the phone call incident, but not at any time did I mention what I had heard nor ask them to explain what had been said in the conversation.

I made a wrongful decision, not asking them to explain what I had heard. As a result, the words I heard festered in my soul. My friends noticed how I had distanced myself by not calling as much and answering their texts timely. They questioned me and said, "What's wrong? Why are you acting so differently by not calling or responding to our texts like you used to?"

They indicated how hurt they felt because we had built a friendship and a bond strong enough that I should have been comfortable to ask them anything. We had made a promise early on in our friendship that if something was bothering us concerning the other person, we would have a discussion.

My friends were so hurt that they said they had lost all trust in me. I then informed them I had overheard their conversation, and based on that conversation, I didn't feel I was the friend they needed. They were appalled I had the audacity to have such an undesirable mindset. They were upset that I even questioned their authentic feelings for me. Wow, I had to take a seat back. I then thought to myself, are you that insecure that you are questioning those who had shown you love, given you the utmost respect. At this moment, I realized I still had no control. However, I had to get a handle on my emotions because they were causing me to become angry with my friends. I then thought you can't dump your negative feelings on others. You must question yourself and set goals to strengthen positive emotions, so you're very comfortable in your skin, so those uncontrollable emotions don't trigger negative actions.

How will you control your emotions ?

List 5 to 10 Things That Trigger Your Emotions

CHAPTER TEN

Don't Feel Invisible

Do you ever feel invisible, meaning someone does not acknowledge anything you say? For example, you are somewhat of an expert regarding a subject matter, or you have a great deal of experience pertaining to that subject matter, but when trying to advise the person, he/she does not acknowledge one thing you say. Why does this happen to you? When you're recovering from a loss of a relationship, it's best you never compromise yourself to feeling invisible because you lose your strength when you need to be strong while coping with the loss.

Who makes you feel invisible the most? Is it friends or family? I have been told that the people you have the most history with sometimes will never see your value when it comes to you having experience of being a subject matter expert in an area. So, you shouldn't be alarmed or feel discouraged. Don't put your head in the sand. Always keep being who you are.

Write Down the People Who Make You Feel Invisible. Next to Their Names, Identify Them as Family, Friends, Co-workers, Etc.

Jot Down the Situations in Which You Were Made to Feel Invisible

Tell How the Situations Made You Feel

How Are You Going to Prepare Yourself for the Next Situation?

CHAPTER ELEVEN
Exert Confidence

As I moved into a new chapter of my life, I immediately was empowered to accomplish additional goals I had yet completed. The feeling I had was unexplainable because I moved with intention and then acted without thinking about the "What If's" or the "Can I's." This attitude gave me a new boldness and a strength of confidence to know who I am and what I want. Confidence is the power of knowing who you are and what you want. Confidence is the power to make things happen which builds your happiness immensely. I read somewhere there are 3 types of people: those who watch things happen; those who make things happen; and those who sit on the sidelines and wonder, saying to themselves what happened. You want to be the person who has the confidence of making things happen which contributes to your growth in confidence. When you're able to build your confidence, it makes your journey of overcoming a loss so much more to overcome.

I thought to myself, I must secure my son and myself. I said to myself, I'm going back to school to get my bachelor's. At that very moment, I got online, applied, and requested information. I then requested my high school transcript and my previous college transcripts because I had already earned my Associate of Applied Science degree. My mind had clicked with a "want," and I immediately acted as if I had to have a taste of something like ice cream with cookies or chocolate, not worrying about how many calories I would consume. I made an immediate decision to go back to school without the thought of the cost. My confidence level was off the charts. I didn't consult or ask for anyone else's opinion. I just did it! I was determined because I knew with the Grace of God it was left up to me to make it happen.

That's what confidence is, believing that you can do things without the opinions of others, being spontaneous. Confidence is also going with your gut instinct because you know yourself, and again not getting the approval from outside sources. No one knows you better than you! No one can be you better than you! So, when you step out and act on your own intuition, you're working with your faith and spiritual realm. God wants us to have faith in ourselves, especially when He has already blessed us with the tools to accomplish and succeed in our destiny. You can go far beyond your wildest thoughts as far as where you want to position yourself during your next journey. So, gain your confidence because this is a step in the process of overcoming your loss and moving on to your next journey.

Exert Confidence

- **C**overed by Grace
- **O**vertly Show Happiness
- **N**ever Giving Up
- **F**earing Nothing
- **I**ndependence Over All Decisions
- **D**estiny - Having Purpose
- **E**xcuses - Don't Own Them
- **N**urturing of the Soul
- **C**reativity of Self
- **E**nergy of Excellence

List How You Exert Confidence.

CHAPTER TWELVE

Affirm Yourself

From whom do you want to affirm? Is it from your mom, dad, siblings, spouse, lover, or best friends etc.? How does it feel when you do not get affirmation when expected?

What did you do when there was a situation in which you didn't get affirmed and, perhaps, you felt hurt? How did you overcome the feeling? I'm here to tell you if you've experienced this feeling, it's okay because if no one has ever told you how to get over it, I will. First, did you know you are your Numero Uno, Number one cheerleader?

No one can make you feel good or cheer for you better than yourself. If you're waiting for someone to pat you on the back or give you affirmations, you may never receive them, and you'll miss out on your purpose. Therefore, when you do something nice for someone, do it for your own gratification. Second, you are the one who must give affirming words and dialog to yourself. No one can affirm you better than yourself and your almighty Deity. He says you're strong, prosperous, and faithful, and He prevents you from being surrounded by negativity. When you're surrounded by negativity, it becomes part of your DNA. It'll stay attached until you change your mindset to positive thoughts. So, start today looking in the mirror and making affirmations. You'll be amazed how confident and focused you'll become every day as you strive to overcome your loss.

    I now live for my own affirmations. I look at the mirror daily and tell myself, "I'm beautiful, strong, smart, loving, kind, graceful, direct, poised, and powerful, and I always show up and show out. I am a breath of fresh air and the life to any party." These are just a few I tell myself which make me feel awesome.

Now That You Are Focused, What Are Your Personal Affirmations?

CHAPTER THIRTEEN

Limit Your Usage of social media

When overcoming a loss such as a relationship, it's best to limit your usage of social media. Begin by temporarily taking a break from all social media platforms. This is to prevent you from being tempted to seeing the person with whom you severed the relationship; that's if the individual is on social media. Checking social media daily can be harmful and detrimental to your health. Just the activity of viewing various comments can have a harmful effect on your mental health. As a result, this can slow down your recovery from the loss. You can become depressed and pessimistic. You may feel a sense of loneliness and rejection just from viewing the social media platforms. So, stop and take some time to break from the platforms, removing people from your list of followers who have shown no support. By following the actions given, you will save yourself from heartache and pain.

When you return to posting on social media, post for a purpose. Don't look for comments from those with whom you have cut ties. If you're looking for a reaction, stop! Do it today. The only person who should be concerned about your post is you! No one must pay attention to your post but you!

A lesson I've learned is just because people don't Like or Comment on your post doesn't mean they're not watching. Remember you're always on stage. People are always watching. People may not react but know they're always watching and paying attention to your posts. When they don't react, you may feel hurt, which will affect your mental well-being and the ability for you to overcome your loss, but don't let their failure to interact with you impede your recovery from your loss, and don't take it personally. Many times, when you're online, people just want to see how consistent you are before they interact with your post. They still may not Like or Comment, but they may send you an instant message.

Also, the people who don't interact may be people you've known since high school and with whom you have never had a formal personal relationship.

As a result, they may perceive you as being that person they defined you to be in high school. So, in that regard, they really don't know you or even know your gifts to even try to respond or interact with you because you're doing things that they didn't expect you to do. The character they defined doesn't match what they're seeing displayed. This can be a huge reason why they don't Like or Comment. They don't know you.

You could conduct a survey to determine why people don't Comment to your posts to determine if they should remain on your platform. When you discuss an event, personally interview people who have stated, "Oh, I saw your pictures." Ask them why they didn't Like or Comment on your photos. Advise them you're doing analytics on why people, such as family especially, may see your postings but never take the time to Like or Comment. Is it because that's something they don't do or they're not comfortable doing, or they don't know how you will feel or react? What is the real reason?

I recently asked 235 people that follow me on Facebook, my Friends & Family to take a survey relating to social media usage. Not surprisingly, only 25 people responded. The answers to the survey questions didn't reflect how the respondents had responded to my social media posts previously created. Although the individuals who took this survey took the time to complete it, their actions didn't reflect that they had ever Liked or Commented on my posts since the inception of my Facebook account. They had neither Liked nor Commented to my post often or never at all.

How ironic was this observation or experiment? Read the survey questions and write down your analysis. Next time you post something that's important to you, take inventory and see how important others, especially family members, add a Comment or hit a Like.

My Survey and Responses

In a typical week, about how often do you Like other Facebook users' activities? The survey results showed 32% stated very often.

How often do you Like or Comment on family posts? The survey results showed 32% stated very often.

When you are on social networking websites like Facebook or Instagram, about how much of your time do you spend looking at what other people have posted? The survey results showed 44% stated most of the time.

How often is a person's brand impactful if you Like or Comment on a post? The survey results showed 28% stated somewhat often.

In a typical month, about how often do you Comment or Like on other Facebook users' activities? The survey results showed 36% stated very often.

On a few occasions, I've been with family and friends, and I've mentioned something or an event I attended, and they'll say, "Oh, I saw your pictures." I then become startled because they didn't Like or Comment on the photos or the post, but they took time to look, paying attention to details. Has that ever happened to you when you've made a fabulous post or picture, and you see an individual, especially a family member, days or maybe weeks later, and he/she mentions in conversation the event or something you have posted and say, "Oh, I saw your pictures," but the individual didn't Like and Comment on one picture or post?

How did that reaction make you feel? Did you follow-up and ask the person why he/she didn't Like your post? If you have people on your friends' list who never ever Like or Comment or they follow you on Instagram as well and never Like or Comment, you want to evaluate why you're still giving them privileges to have access to what's going on in your life. You may also want to think about removing them from your platform. Removing people from your platform list can be the most rewarding action ever because it's like pruning a tree to remove all the dead branches not adding value to grow new branches. Know right at this moment you can create a list of a few people you need to remove to help you continue with your recovery. For example, if it's your birthday and those folks can't even acknowledge you, remove them, pruning away those dead branches. Now, take a moment and take inventory of your friends' list on all social media platforms and begin to prune. Lastly, if you have anyone on your list like persons from a broken friendship, those individuals should be first on your list to remove.

Once you've pruned your social media, just continue to do and be who you are and keep shining. Keep using social media for your purposes – to inform and inspire through your postings or stories.

I've limited the time spent on social media and only posted what's important to me without concentrating on others who have never supported me or have helped me overcome a loss. I've been able to be strong, not even thinking of that relationship that was lost but gaining and sharing information and its benefits that are important to me and the community.

CHAPTER FOURTEEN

Do Not Compromise Yourself

You must never compromise yourself, give your power to someone else without regards to how you are feeling, becoming vulnerable. When subjecting yourself to vulnerability, you can become distracted, confused, and disoriented when trying to maintain your peaceful well-being for your new journey. Have you ever been in a situation where you compromised yourself, in which you were made to feel like crawling under a rock or tucking your head in like a turtle when it goes back in its shell? I mean have you ever endured someone taking out his/her frustrations on you when in fact you have no idea why, nor do you know the individual is upset. You know you haven't intentionally tried to hurt the individual, but the negative energy is directed towards you. Can you think of a time when this has happened to you? When it did happen, were you able to walk away or were you in a confined place like a car, bus, train, or plane and you just had no physical control to walk away? What did you do in this situation? Were you able to leave the environment?

I've been in a situation in which there was so much negative energy towards me that there was absolutely nothing I could do. I felt like a helpless child without a parent or guardian. As a grown woman at that moment, I, as a passenger in a car, had no easy exit. I was not even in a location in which I could have said pull over and let ME OUT of the car because we were in an area with no sidewalks, no access to busses, and to make things worse, it was a very cold day. At that moment, I had to suck it up and take deep a breath, controlling my anger, keeping myself calm. The individual was non-verbal the entire ride, and that's absolutely the worst feeling ever, to be in a non-verbal tense atmosphere in which you can feel the negative energy. I can tell you it wasn't a good feeling.

What did I learn from this experience? I learned a great deal about myself on that cold winter day. I learned how mentally strong I was because I could've easily snapped. But I stayed calm, realizing I had done nothing wrong to create the situation. Since that day, I've also thought about what I could've done not to have been in that situation. Looking back, I realize that when I noticed the tension before the driver took off, I could've made my exit out of the car, advising I have had a change of plans and then exiting the vehicle politely. This was a very good lesson which says never let your feelings be compromised by anyone ever. Individuals don't have the right to make you feel uncomfortable because they're having a bad day or suspect you did something intentionally to hurt their feelings.

If an individual can't communicate his/her feelings at that moment, then you should immediately remove yourself from that environment to avoid being vulnerable. To stay in such an environment, you'll become vulnerable to painful feelings. You deserve better, so again never compromise yourself or well-being. To not compromise is a source of being your authentic self because at this point, you're always aware what you will or will not tolerate.

Because of this awareness, I say to you start thinking of exit plans if or when this should ever happen. I hope you'll never experience this situation. Again, stay calm and be conscious as to what's going on when or if it happens, so you're not caught off guard.

As one can see, to protect your sanity during the recovery from your loss, you can't compromise yourself because it leads to vulnerability. As a result, you'll become depressed and have a sense of loneliness. This action will also become a setback in your bouncing back to your strong authentic self.

Jot Down the Situations in Which You Felt Compromised

Tell What You Did When Feeling Compromised

CHAPTER FIFTHTEEN

Be Content

After the loss, you may feel alone, but it's ok to be alone. A wise man once asked me, "How does it feel being alone, being by yourself, meaning not having a male companion around to talk to on a consistent basis?" The wise man also asked, "Do you ever get bored?" I told him I have grown not to have a feeling of loneliness or boredom. I call this being content with myself and being able to love and have tolerance for myself when being alone. If you don't like being with yourself, how do you expect others to be around you or treat you with dignity and respect? I wasn't always comfortable with being by myself. I remember when I was younger, under 30 years of age, I would go out to clubs, concerts, etc. to prevent being at home alone. I wasn't always comfortable with being by myself. I had a hard time staying still, being content, and being by myself. I didn't know the power of spending valuable time with myself.

Today things are much different. When I'm alone, I read, exercise, and listen to some of my motivational speakers. I also enjoy meditating and learning more of who I really am while understanding my purpose in life. As a result of spending time by myself, I've learned that it's okay to be alone. A spouse, lover, or friend, if you have either of those, doesn't make you whole; knowing yourself makes you whole. I recommend that you try some of the activities that I enjoy.

When being alone, persons can tap into their spiritual self and learn the heartbeat of their souls. I'm content with being myself, not trying to mimic someone else, but running my own race, while living out my own purpose.

CHAPTER SIXTEEN

Live Vibrantly

Now that you are content being alone, it is time for you to live vibrantly. What does live vibrantly mean to you? It means being full of energy with enthusiasm. How you look, how you get up in the morning, and how you apply self-care to yourself play a role in your feeling vibrant.

Another key to live vibrantly after a loss is to wake up every day wanting to feel beautiful. When you look good, you feel good, thriving even more to ensure self-care when getting over a loss. Some people like to wear sweats or jeans, and some women don't wear make-up. Whatever you decide to wear, make sure it's spunky, clean, and vibrant because when it's spunky, clean, and vibrant, you'll feel beautiful and happy. This is what you should do while embracing your NEW YOU after the loss.

Be beautiful, not for someone else, but for yourself. Make yourself feel beautiful or handsome because at the end of the day, as I mentioned before, you can only make yourself happy. Nobody can make you happy but you, nobody can make you beautiful or handsome but you, and nobody can light up a room being vibrant but you, so I say today do you! Don't worry about what others think. Be who you want to be, which is vibrant, and do whatever makes you vibrant. Do you! I am telling you the way you look and the way you feel about yourself will build extreme confidence levels.

 Discern what you need to be beautiful. Go shopping and buy the things you need. Re-up on your clothing, picking up desirable pieces that are attractive to the eyes. Even though you may not be in the dating arena, this is for you. Be desirable for yourself; feel desirable for yourself, as you never have before. Attractive clothing will boost your confidence immensely. There is nothing like feeling good in your clothes. When you feel and look good, you reflect positive feelings externally. After you have bought new clothing, clean out your closets. You will be surprised at what you find. Get rid of any items you haven't worn in a year or more. I would suggest donating the items to a non-profit agency from which you can obtain a write off. As a result, if you don't first take care of the unwanted clothing, this will slow down the momentum of your becoming whole with more energy, enthusiasm, and self-care. It is necessary that you make room for the new.

Now that we're done with clothing, let's turn our attention to haircare. Do you like your hair color as it is today? I say try a new hair color that makes a statement. Step out of your comfort zone and try something new. Get rid of the familiar.

Many times, we can't grow unless we've tried something that's not comfortable. You'll be surprised how a small change will make you feel and even surprise those around you who will witness your boldness and take notice. Remember you're always on stage, meaning people are always looking. As a result, you're an inspiration. Even when you think no one is paying attention, trust me they're watching.

Your new look will draw positive attention from others who want to now inherit your transformation and positive energy. When there's a change and it's noticeable, some people may want a piece of the experience. I can remember a time when I dyed and cut my hair. I felt like a trendsetter because associates followed, at least those who were in my daily presence. How do you think that made me feel? I felt like an empowered, phenomenal woman.

Now let's talk about skincare. Be sure to drink your daily average of water because it purifies you, giving you healthy skin. When you drink water, it brings a glow to your skin, and it helps weight maintenance. Make sure you note the average body intake for water. To determine how many ounces you need, take your weight in pounds and multiply by 2/3 or 67% to determine the average amount of water you should drink daily.

Finding a hobby will also help you to live vibrantly. One of my hobbies is journaling which provides many of the same benefits as working out. I get emotional when journaling because it takes away my stress.

List Your Hobbies.

In addition to enjoying hobbies, what's on your bucket list? Plan the trip of your dreams. Once you plan where you want to go, hire a travel agent to alleviate any anxiety in planning the trip. Ask family or friends to go with you. If they say no, don't worry. Don't let the no prevent you from booking the trip of your dreams. You will not have to wonder or have the "what ifs." When the trip is all booked, you'll immediately feel empowered. By sticking to your travel plans, you'll ultimately empower others to follow your lead because it'll show your strength in executing your plan. Now, let's get ready and get excited to have some fun.

My other suggestion is engaging in the arts. Engaging in the arts once a week, every other week, or monthly is therapy to the Mind, Body, and Soul.

Here are some activities to consider:

- Visit an Art Museum
- Attend Plays
- Listen to Various Genres of Music

- Attend Festivals

Engaging in the various arts can elicit some interests that you probably had no idea you had. It can help you mentally with having the capacity of directing your energy elsewhere, which is therapeutic. It's like when you take time out to exercise or go shopping; these activities can be therapeutic to some people. These are just a few examples to empower and uplift your spirits without fear.

Power Over Fear = Tenacity

I challenge you to experience some of the arts in the next 30 days. I want you to journal your experience when you participate in the arts as well as when you go on vacation. Your vacation doesn't have to be 7 to 10 days; it can be a 3-day mini vacation. Just do it; don't make any excuses. Enjoy your getaway. Relax, rejuvenate, and refocus on what really is important in your life. It's time that you take a break from all the hustle and bustle, leaving it all behind for the moment. Then once you're back from vacation, you're rejuvenated.

If you follow these tips, you're on your way to a recovery after your loss with a burst of rejuvenation that will remain consistent in your life with fullness.

CHAPTER SEVENTEEN

Enjoy Friendships

When you've gone through a loss, such as a divorce, it's important to enjoy friends. You want to ensure you're protecting your well-being and not moving too quickly, especially if it's related to dating. However, it's healthy to begin developing new friendships. Do you have any close friends or a companion? I dare you to have at least one in your life. This will create balance, joy, and more love in your life. We all need someone with whom we can just share our most intimate feelings. To be able to share what's on our minds and have the listening ear of another person without judgment is healthy. It's not healthy to keep your emotions and thoughts bottled; it brings about fear and loneliness.

Being alone may cause mental stress, and it also causes stress on your body. When you have undue stress, this can cause all types of internal illnesses and diseases, such as hypertension, obesity, sleep deprivation, and many other illnesses or even viruses. Therefore, you must focus on making yourself happy and engaging in creative personal activities that give you fulfillment.

Your happiness is important to your mental health because it controls the amount of stress your body endures over a period. If your mental well-being is not balanced, you'll have a hard time coping with any unforeseen circumstances that may appear in your life. So, I say to you let's get started and find a friend. Have you lost communication with friends who were once in your life? Do you recall how you lost contact? I suggest you give them a call and see what they have been doing. Plan a luncheon or activity where you and your friends can get together to learn, review, or share the events that have occurred in your lives. You'll be amazed just how refreshing this act of kindness will make you feel. Commit to planning and doing more activities with friends. Having a plan keeps you focused without distraction for doing activities with your friends.

Today you're going to start writing in a planner. If you're already doing so, great. If you don't have a planner, purchase one today as soon as possible to ensure you have a plan for your activities. Now, I want you to meditate on fun things you would like to do in your city that you and your friends can do without a notice or reservation.

Make a List of Things to Do with Your Friends.

In your planner, document your hours and the best day to visit according to your schedule of activities you have occurring in your life. Once you complete this activity, you're on your way to a more fruitful life. You shouldn't have a dull moment in your life again.

After Completing This Activity, How Do You Feel?

You should feel empowered because you'll always be in control of your time because you're in the driver's seat in managing everything you do with your friends. Being surrounded with friends will ease your recovery from your loss.

CHAPTER EIGHTEEN

Establish a New Relationship Cautiously

If you're overcoming a relationship loss, you may want to establish new relationships, but be cautious. How do you define the word relationship? I define the word in two parts. When someone is in a **"RELATION,"** he/she has a basic friendship with someone; he/she has only shared a third of a layer of an onion. I will talk about this in more detail towards the end of this chapter.

The **"SHIP"** of the word indicates your partner is accountable for responsibilities he or she has for the relationship. When there is no **"SHIP,"** meaning actions of responsibility from the other individual, you don't have a committed relationship; you have nothing. It's like a half full glass of water or a half glass of supposedly sweet tea with no sugar.

If you can define any **"RELATIONS"** you have with an individual by using my definition of what a relationship means, the word **"SHIP"** will give you clarity at a 360-degree view if there's going to be longevity or failure. If I had followed this analogy before my failed relations, I would have prevented a great deal of self-inflicting heartaches. But this was something I learned after my experience. Yes, I call the heartache self-inflicting because the red flags I experienced I chose to ignore. Sometimes you go through things to help others who may be going through similar situations prevent heartache but gain awareness. Remember it's never too late to change, and you're never too old to learn something new like a methodology to help uncover truth and awareness.

  Be aware that there're signs that the relationship will not work out. It's like trying to force a circle in a square peg; the action never works. Scientifically, if you try to force something that will not fit, it'll never go the course because it's not aligned with nature; it'll always go against nature.

  Here's a great example when two people don't fit in a relationship. In the beginning, you both knew something didn't feel right; however, you both became enablers to one another's issues. You may not have been aware of what the other person may have been concealing.

For example, when you meet someone and you begin to date, and for the first 6 months, you feel like "I know this person." Do you think you really know the individual? I've found out when dating someone or even being married, getting to know a person is like peeling away an onion that has layers. Imagine a bare onion before it's cut. Close your eyes and picture the onion; think of its image, how it feels and smells once you peel and cut it. Now what do you see? Well, I'll tell you just what I've seen and even experienced with the onion. The onion has layers upon layers, and when you think you're at the core, there's another layer to peel away. When dealing with an individual, you'll see that one has many layers; even you have many layers. Anyone can attest that when you begin learning about someone you're falling in love with, you'll realize he/she has layers.

You may think you know everything about that person, and then something happens when you find out later you do not know that person 100%. Do you feel it's wrong to not know someone at 100%? I say no because we're all human beings, and we all have some insecurities we may just want to keep to ourselves and only share with our creator, even taking them to our graves, which is perfectly fine. When discovering and noticing you don't know the individual fully, don't become loosely vulnerable.

For example, when the individual does something unusual that's a huge surprise, don't' sweat it; add it to your file. Don't let your emotions take hold of you. Just count your blessings that something has been uncovered to help you make a decision. You may be ok with the news, or the news may ultimately force you to break off the relationship. Again, keep your emotions in check and don't totally fall apart.

A rule of thumb is to always prepare yourself for not knowing 100% of an individual with whom you have a relationship. It's like the 80/20 rule, meaning you may know a good 20%, and 80% you just don't know, or you can switch the numbers to be 80/20. Regardless, the logic still equals 100% of you not knowing everything.

Therefore, you must have an attitude of self-worth which means you'll never neglect yourself or harbor someone else's insecurities to make him/her feel great. If you always put yourself first, regardless of what that person is keeping from you, nothing can ever destroy you or your happiness. Always remember you're in control of your own happiness and destiny. If someone is dealing with something inside of himself or herself, at times it can keep him/her unhappy. This is something you can't control, and again those are layers that you may or may not know, depending upon how much time you're dedicating to that person. I feel it can take a lifetime to get to know someone. Even then, the individual can leave this earth with secrets about him/herself and unknown feelings for you going with him/her to the grave.

Although you may not know a person 100%, when establishing a new romantic relationship, try to learn if the person wants you. There's nothing more powerful than someone wanting you in his/her life as much as you want him/her in your life. To be cautious in a relationship is to want what wants you to ensure the person wants the same thing you want. Sometimes when we have experienced a loss, we tend to overtly jump ahead of committing to a relationship with someone without getting a **commitment**.

Before committing to a relationship, determine if the individual is interested in being in a relationship. Ask yourself are you the one who always initiates the line of contact, such as a call, a text, or an email. To test this theory, do one of the following three things. First, make a phone call. If your call goes to a voicemail, and you don't get a callback within 24 to 48 hours, you aren't a priority. Second, send a text message and track the length of time it takes for a response. If you don't get a response within minutes or at least within an hour or get no response at all, you aren't a priority. This indicates the individual does not value you as a person or an important human being. Lastly, send a card such as a Thinking of You. If you don't get an acknowledgement within 7 to 10 days or more after the card has been mailed, you're not a priority, and the individual to whom you sent the card just really doesn't acknowledge or value you as someone with whom he/she would like to create a long-term relationship.

I have tested this theory, and I was excited about the results because they showed me if the individual was interested in being in a relationship, and I learned it is ok if the individual didn't respond to my cards because it validated my theory of being a priority. It made me feel more relaxed to release a person out of my life who didn't want to be a part of my circle. I say to you want what wants you, and if someone doesn't want to be in your circle, it is ok. He/she may have a different expectation of the relationship than you have. You may picture the individual as a new romantic love interest. You must be careful when attaching a label to a new friend because it may be one with which he/she may not agree. You may feel the new friend is the ideal mate and begin to start making plans for your future without involving the individual in the conversation of the thought process. While on the other hand, your ideal mate may see you as a friend, someone to spend time with, but nothing more serious than just being a friend with no long-term commitments.

    Take the time to study and learn the individual. When you're going through this process, it will not take long at all to know if the individual has the same feelings. This process is cautionary when recovering from a loss to obtain a committed new relationship.

What is your ideal Friendship or Relationship

CHAPTER NINETEEN

Give Thanks

Do you ever take the time to be thankful for what you have? Do you ever take the time to be thankful for being alive? You will be surprised how many people don't take the time to take inventory of their lives. I think this is because we get caught up with our day-to-day activities, not realizing we have a lot to be grateful for. In return, we are worried about progressing to our next destination. So many of us have so much disposable income or disposable resources that we're just not thankful.

Although you have experienced a loss, take inventory, and think about why you should be grateful for what you have. I'm thankful for having peace of mind and my health. Finally, take a step back; think about exactly what you want and how it will be obtainable. While doing this process, you will become more grateful and appreciative for those things you do own. As a result, you'll slow down trying to get the things you want because you'll become thankful for all

that you have in your life.

What are You Thankful For?

Realizing what you are thankful for makes you happy and builds character, self-confidence, and self-esteem. You come to realize that if you didn't get one more item in your life, you would be just fine. If you're thankful, you'll be blessed with more. You'll be blessed with the fulfillment of a goal that you've been working to accomplish. Have you ever worked hard at something like passing a test or trying to obtain that position you wanted and didn't get it? What happened when you made the first attempt? Did you fail the first time? If this happened to you, what did you do? Did you cry and give up, quitting by not attempting to try a second or third or even a fourth time? If you answer yes to any one of the questions, you've completely failed yourself. You've given up on yourself, and you begin to play mind games with self-negative talk. STOP. Don't self-sabotage yourself. Decide what you did wrong and take a moment to access all the good things about yourself and the resources you have already to be great. As you continue to work towards your goal, know that you will be blessed in accomplishing your goal because you are thankful.

CHAPTER TWENTY

My Prayer

Father God, I come to You giving You all praises. I thank You for letting me share to my readers what You have given me. I thank You, Father God, for my five senses, especially my hands that are typing these words at the moment so they can be read by people around the world. You are an almighty God that sits up high and looks down low. I thank You for letting me bring all my concerns and thoughts to just You in my presence. Father God, I love and trust our communication so much that I dare not utter a word to anyone. Father God, I love when I'm going through something, you have my back and pat me on my back to say, "Fear not; do not worry." Father God, it has been humbling knowing I have only had You to talk to when questioning why I am going through issues in life that make me feel uncomfortable. Father God, I feel good knowing I do not have to ask someone else's opinion about any situation.

I have learned to be humble seeking You out loud and in meditation, waiting to hear Your voice or spiritual calm to comfort me during the day or in the midnight hour. Father God, I love You because You are my strength when I am weak; You are my counselor of reasoning; and You are my mind, body, and soul in the rim of my gut of uncertainty. Father God, I thank You for holding it all together for me, so I do not worry or fret what comes before me. For all the blessings, security, and comfort You have given me, Father God, I say thank You, thank You, thank You; I cannot say thank You enough. Father God, the strong power that You have provided, allowing me to drop everything, relieving the weight of my body and soul, has humbled me to my core.

I know you have blessed me to give something to readers in this book to use or to tuck in their toolbox of life. I know they are stronger in their body, mind, and the gut rim of their souls. I know they know who they are and who they are working to become. Father

God, I pray they have boldness, confidence, and tenacity, not worrying about getting any affirmations from man or woman but only from You, Father God. Now, Father God, keep us wrapped in Your arms with hundreds and thousands of legends of angels so we can maneuver our lives, whether the situations be big or small.

Made in the USA
Columbia, SC
09 June 2024